DATE DUE		
JY 26 '89		
AG 31 '89		
JUL 13 '94		
FEB 17 '95		
AP 18 '00		
AG 14 03		
FE 27 '8		

UNDER THE GROUND

ANDREW LANGLEY

The Bookwright Press
New York · 1986

Topics

The Age of the Dinosaurs
Great Disasters
Under the Ground

All the words that appear
in **bold** are explained in the
glossary on page 30.

First published in the United States in 1986 by
The Bookwright Press
387 Park Avenue South
New York NY 10016

First published in 1985 by
Wayland (Publishers) Ltd
61 Western Road, Hove
East Sussex BN3 1JD

ISBN 0–531–18049–2
Library of Congress Catalog Card Number: 85–71730

Phototypeset by Kalligraphics Ltd
Redhill, Surrey, England
Printed by G. Canale & C.S.p.A., Turin, Italy

Contents

Animals Underground

If you dig into a piece of turf, you are sure to find an earthworm. In every acre of grassland there live as many as a million worms. They tunnel through the soil, swallowing it as they go, and taking out the food they need. What they don't need is left behind as **earthworm castings**.

In this way they move many tons of soil on the earth's surface. Rocks and other large objects are slowly buried by their work. The prehistoric

These coiled heaps of soil are earthworm castings, the waste left behind by worms.

See how damp and shiny these worms are.

stones of Stonehenge in England are being covered up at the rate of 20 cm (8 inches) every century. But the tunneling is good for the soil, letting in air and helping water to drain away.

Worms spend most of their lives underground. They must stay damp and cool, and the sun quickly dries them up. Besides, they have enemies above ground – thrushes, starlings and other birds who will pull them up and eat them.

Moles have very long, sharp claws that help them to tunnel through the earth.

There are also enemies below. Moles dig long tunnels in the soil and wait for their food to drop into them. They eat a large number of worms: one mole eats at least fifty worms each day.

Many larger animals live underground because of the safety it gives them. Rabbits may be attacked by foxes or birds of prey, so they dig burrows. Each burrow has at least two entrance holes. If an enemy

A rabbit peeps out of his burrow to see if it is safe to come out and feed.

comes near, the rabbit thumps on the ground with its hind feet to warn others of danger, and then runs below.

These gerbils are sleeping in the cool sand of their burrow in the Namib Desert.

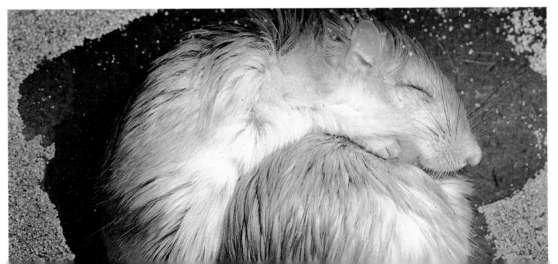

The earth protects animals from many other dangers, too. In the desert the sun is so hot at midday that nothing can live for long on the surface. But, only a few inches down, the sand is cool. Many creatures bury themselves in the sand during the day. They come out to feed at night.

The Spadefoot toad, so named because it can dig deep into the ground, only comes out of its hole after heavy rain.

The spadefoot toad stays deep in its hole for many months at a time. It does not eat or drink. By staying completely still it does not use up any energy or water. Only when there has been heavy rain does it emerge. In a few hours it feeds, lays its eggs and burrows back into the sand again to wait for another year.

Cold can be just as dangerous as heat. Even the polar bear, with its thick fur, has to find shelter underground during the harsh Arctic winter. The young bears are born in caves under the ice, safe from the freezing winds.

A hole in the ground is the perfect place for an ambush. The purse spider digs out a thin tube, and covers the opening with a purse, or web, of silk. Then it waits at the bottom of the tube. As soon as an insect lands on the purse, the spider rushes up and kills it. Then it pulls the insect down through the silk and eats it. Later, the purse has to be mended, ready for the next meal.

Some animals live so deep underground that they never see daylight. In Hawaii, the lava flowing from volcanoes has left long tunnels. Many strange insects, among them spiders and beetles, live in these tunnels. Because of the darkness they do not need to see, and so they have no eyes. Instead, they have long legs and antennae which help them to feel around for food.

The Riches of the Earth

Parts of the earth's surface were made by **volcanoes** and **earthquakes**. Red hot **lava** poured out of cracks and cooled in layers, which were folded and crushed. The heat and weight caused the rock to be changed into different kinds of **minerals**.

One of the most important minerals is iron. It is strong and hard, but can be melted and shaped easily. With other metals, such as aluminum, it can be used for making anything from an ocean liner to a penknife. Some minerals are called "precious"

A precious lump! – gold ore found in Montana.

This flint hand-ax was made and used thousands of years ago.

because they are so beautiful and hard to find. Gems, such as diamonds, and metals, such as gold and silver, are "precious" and very valuable.

We have been using these minerals for many centuries to make tools and weapons. When we saw how useful they were, we looked for more. But of course most minerals are buried deep underground. Some are mixed with other rock, called ore. Others are found in layers, called seams.

So mining began. Nearly 5,000 years ago, people in England dug for flint. Their pits were not very deep, because they had no way of keeping the sides from collapsing. They used flint to light fires by striking two pieces together, which made sparks. Flint was also made into ax heads. The first people to dig deep shafts were the Romans. They lined the walls with timber and drained the water out with buckets. One of their mines was over 300 meters (990 feet) deep.

Modern mines go down much farther than that. When diamonds were discovered at Kimberley in South Africa, the miners went on digging for more than 1,000 meters (3,300 feet). The "Big Hole," as it is called, is the deepest ever made by man.

Coal is found in seams which are usually a long way underground. A **shaft** is sunk straight down until the seam is reached. From here a tunnel is dug, following the line of the coal. The roof of the tunnel

The roof of this tunnel in a coal mine in West Virginia is too low for the miners to walk upright.

A coal miner watches a shearer in operation.

is held up by steel props that must be carefully checked every day. Seams that are close to the surface can be mined by the **opencast** or **strip** method. This involves clearing away the topsoil to expose the coal, which can then easily be dug out.

There are two ways of mining the coal found deep underground. One is to drill holes in the coal face and fill them with explosives. When these are set off they break up the face into pieces. The other way is to cut the face with a big machine called a shearer. The pieces of coal are loaded onto conveyor belts or trains and taken back to the main shaft. Then they are hoisted to the surface.

This oil drilling platform in the North Sea is burning off gas found below the sea-bed.

Oil also lies underground, but it does not have to be dug up. A drilling platform is built over the place where the oil lies. This may be on land or out at sea. When a hole is drilled into the deposit, the oil can be pumped out. It is fed through a pipe to a refinery, where it is turned into gasoline and other fuels.

Where there is oil underground there may be gas, too. This can also be used as a fuel. If there is a gas stove in your house, it probably burns natural gas. A rotten smell, called a "stench," is added to gas so that you will know when it is leaking.

Two thousand tons of coal an hour are dug out of this opencast mine in Australia.

Caves and Tunnels

The earth beneath our feet is far from solid. Aside from mines, there are naturally made cracks and caverns. Sometimes there are whole networks of caves leading into each other. These caves are found in many parts of the world, especially where there is **limestone** rock.

Limestone is easily worn away by water. When the rain or a stream finds a crack, it will run down into the rock. The water searches out the weak points underground and slowly hollows out tunnels. As the walls and ceilings fall in, the tunnels grow bigger. Many are big enough for us to walk into. Cave explorers, equipped with strong lights and ropes, can travel long distances in this strange world.

People build tunnels for different purposes. The first ones were used for carrying water. In AD 41 the Romans dug a tunnel to drain Lake Fucino. The work was done by slaves, who hacked their way through 6 km (3½ miles) of solid rock using only picks and shovels. Many of them died because there was not enough air to breathe underground.

Later engineers made sure that plenty of fresh air came into their tunnels. In 1766, a man called James Brindley built a tunnel in England. He put braziers of burning coal in each shaft. The heat from the coal pulled air into the tunnel. Brindley was also able to use gunpowder, which made the work easier. The explosions broke up the rock, which was carried out in trucks. But whenever he struck an underground stream the tunnel filled up with water. This had to be taken out by a steam pump.

Inside a limestone cavern, a cave explorer wonders at the shapes of rocks formed over many years.

*These cars are traveling through the road tunnel
under the Huangpu River in China.*

Many tunnels were being built in the 1800s for
roads, canals and railroads. One of the longest was
through Mont Cenis in the Alps. It was started in
1857. At first, work was very slow because the rock
was so hard. Then the workmen began using drills
which were powered by **compressed air**, and the
great tunnel was finished in fourteen years. It is still
in use today.

In 1825, Marc Brunel was asked to dig a tunnel
underneath the Thames River in London. He knew
that there were terrible dangers in digging near
running water. The ground was made of soft silt
and mud that often collapsed. Tons of water
flooded through any weak spot.

The London subway system, or "tube," carries millions of people under London's busy streets every day.

Brunel made a huge shield. This was moved forward with the tunnel face as it was being dug. It held up the ceiling and protected the men working on the face. This sort of shield has been used for building tunnels ever since.

Modern tunnels have very strong walls. After the rock has been blasted and cleared away, the walls are lined with pieces of cast iron which are bolted together. In some tunnels the ceiling is sprayed with concrete as it is being dug. This holds the rock together and keeps it from falling in.

Today, underground roads and railroads are more important than ever. Millions of people travel to work by subway. Tunnels carry cars and trucks underneath cities quickly and quietly. Without them, our streets would be a lot more crowded.

Pipes and Cables

Each of us uses a lot of water every day. We turn on the faucet and it pours out. When we have finished with it, the water disappears down the drain. But where does it come from, and where does it go?

A bucket has to be lowered down the shaft to get water out of this well.

Here you can see the settling basins of a sewage works in Edmonton, Canada.

The water in our pipes starts out as rain. It falls to the earth and soaks down through **porous** rock such as limestone or chalk. When it reaches a non-porous layer it can go no farther. If it can find a crack, it will flow out as a spring. If not, it will build up into an underground lake.

Once water has been located, a well can be dug down to it. Sometimes these are very deep. One in Ancient China went down to more than 450 meters (1,500 feet). The walls were lined with brick or stone, and the water was drawn up in a bucket. Later, pumps were used which pulled the water up through a pipe.

Today's pumps draw huge quantities of water to the surface. But before it can be sent to our homes it has to be made clean and safe to drink. First it is put into a settling basin, where large pieces of grit or dirt will sink to the bottom. Then it is filtered through sand, which takes out any dirt that is left. Lastly a small amount of **chlorine** is added to kill the germs in the water.

From the cleaning plant, the water is pumped along pipes to our homes. Water pipes are laid

This sewage pipe is more than big enough for a man to walk through.

The pipes that run beneath our streets must be regularly inspected to ensure they are not damaged or blocked.

beneath the streets. The pipe must be at least 75cm (2½ feet) below the surface, so that it won't freeze up in winter.

When we have used the water, it goes back underground. From our drainpipes it flows into a bigger pipe called a sewer. This also runs along beneath the street. There are many miles of sewers under most modern towns. Most are big enough to walk through, and some are as wide as a street. They are all checked regularly to make sure that they are not blocked.

Sewage water is much too dirty to be poured straight into the sea or a river. First of all it has to be purified. It flows into a settling tank and is left to stand. Most of the heavy dirt sinks to the bottom, to make sludge. The water is sprinkled over a bed of gravel which gets rid of the harmful germs. Then it can be pumped away to the sea.

Set into the streets of a town or a city, you may see several metal covers. The cover for the water pipe may have a large "W" on it. The cover for the sewer will be big and heavy. The hole underneath must be wide enough for a person to climb down to inspect the pipes.

Other covers may say "Telephone" or "Electricity." Cables for these services may also be buried under the streets. A trench is dug, 45 to 100 cm (18 to 40 inches) deep, into which a pipe is laid. The cables are fed into the pipe, which is then buried. The pipe protects the cables and allows engineers to locate them easily for repair and replacement. They are much safer and neater there than when they are carried by ugly **pylons** or telegraph poles.

The most up-to-date networks of communications cables to be laid underground are made of glass and are no thicker than a human hair. They are called **optical fibers**. Each optical fiber can carry thousands of telephone calls, television pictures or computer information. Such messages are sent along the cables using pulses of light instead of electricity. These light pulses are made using **lasers**.

These men are busy preparing to lay cables under a street.

Hidden Underground

There are many interesting things hidden under the ground. They are often preserved for many years, because they have not been open to the air, wind or rain. For example, in 1944 the body of a man was found in a peat bog in Denmark. He had lain there since about 100 BC, but most of his clothes had been preserved. By looking at them we can see how men used to dress 2,000 years ago.

In 1940, two boys were walking their dog in the hills near Montignac in southern France. The dog

Many cave walls have been found to have paintings on them. This one was painted by Aborigines in Australia.

The cool darkness of this cellar keeps the barrels of wine from spoiling.

was chasing a rabbit when suddenly he disappeared down a hole. The boys went to look for him, and slid down into a dark cave. As they looked around they were amazed to see that the walls of the cave were covered with paintings.

The paintings, of bulls and other animals, were over 20,000 years old. The still air of the cave had kept them in perfect condition. People from all over the world flocked to see them. However, the crowds brought heat and germs into the cave, and the paintings began to fade. The cave had to be closed up again. Today, tourists can look at copies of the pictures which are on show at the mouth of the cave.

Even more exciting was the discovery, in 1922, of the tomb of the Egyptian King Tutankhamun. An archaeologist was digging in the Valley of the Kings near the Nile River, when he found the tomb. No one had been inside it for 3,000 years.

The king was buried inside four coffins. The outer one was made of stone, and the next two of wood covered in gold. The inner coffin was made of solid gold, and weighed 136 kg (300 lb). Thrones, statues and masks made of gold and silver were also found. The tomb was so full of treasures that it took six years to empty.

We still use cellars under the ground to keep things safe. Banks lock money and other valuable things in their vaults. These have very thick doors which are difficult for a thief to cut open. They also have **combination locks** that do not need keys.

These bank vaults in France are used to keep the country's gold reserves safe.

Egypt's Valley of the Kings is the site of the entrance to Tutankhamun's tomb.

Cellars are perfect places for storing wine. They are cool and dark, which keeps the wine in good condition. In Britain, many bars, or "pubs," keep their beer in cellars as well.

Gasoline can catch fire and explode very easily. The safest place to store it is in huge tanks underground. At a garage you may see a tank truck delivering gasoline for the pumps. It is piped down through a hose into the tanks underneath.

People can find safety underground, too. During World War II, many families had shelters covered with earth to protect them from bombs. In London, thousands of people slept on the platforms of the "Underground" (the subway). In some cities today, many new shelters are being built in case there is another war.

Glossary

Chlorine A chemical used to purify water.

Combination lock A lock that will open only when the numbers on its dial have been set in a special order.

Compressed air Air that is pumped under great pressure and used to drive drills and diggers without any danger of fire.

Earthquake Shock waves in the earth. Earthquakes often cause a lot of damage.

Earthworm casting The small coil of earth left behind by a worm.

Laser A device that gives out a very strong beam of light.

Lava The red-hot and molten rock that flows out of a volcano.

Limestone A rock made up mostly of tiny particles of shells or coral. It is used for building and for making lime.

Mineral One of many kinds of rocks made by the heat of volcanoes or by pressure below the earth's surface.

Porous Having tiny holes that allow water to pass through.

Pylon A steel tower used for carrying electricity cables across the country.

Opencast mining Mining near the surface by clearing away topsoil to expose a mineral.

Shaft A hole dug straight down into the earth, where the building of a mine or tunnel may begin.

Strip mining See opencast mining.

Volcano A weak part of the earth's crust through which molten lava and gases can pour.

Books to read

Constant, Constantine. *The Student Earth Scientist Explores Earth and Its Materials.* New York, NY: Rosen Group, 1975.
Dixon, Dougal. *Geology.* New York: Franklin Watts, 1983.
McGowen, Tom. *Album of Rocks and Minerals.* Chicago, IL: Rand-McNally, 1981.
Morris, Dean. *Animals That Burrow.* Milwaukee, WI: Raintree Publications, 1977.

Index

Picture acknowledgments

British Museum, 20; Bruce Coleman Limited: Rod and Moira Borland, 7 (bottom); Jane Burton, 7 (top); Nicholas Devore, 10; Michael Freeman, 27; C.B. Frith, 26; J.L.G. Grande, 5; Peter Jackson, 29; M.P. Kahl, 8; Hans Reinhard, 6; Roger Wilmhurst, 20; GeoScience Features/J. Wooldridge, cover; Tony Waltham/GEOSLIDES, 17; National Coal Board, 13; PHOTRI, 22, 23, 25; TOPHAM, 4, 12, 21; Xinhua News Agency, 18. All other pictures are from the Wayland Picture Library.